D1710237

The 9/11 TERRORIST ATTACKS

A DAY THAT CHANGED AMERICA

by Amy Maranville

CAPSTONE PRESS

a capstone imprint

Capstone Captivate is published by Capstone Press, an imprint of Capstone.
1710 Roe Crest Drive, North Mankato, Minnesota 56003
www.capstonepub.com

Library of Congress Cataloging-in-Publication Data
Names: Maranville, Amy, author.
Title: The 9/11 terrorist attacks : a day that changed America / by Amy Maranville.
Description: North Mankato, Minnesota : Capstone Captivate, [2022] | Series: Days that changed America | Includes bibliographical references and index. | Audience: Ages 8-11 | Audience: Grades 4-6 | Summary: "On September 11, 2001, an entire country ground to a halt as terrorists attacked the World Trade Center in New York City, the U.S. Pentagon in Washington D.C., and crashed an airliner near Shanksville, Pennsylvania. Now readers can step back in time to learn what led up to the 9/11 terrorist attacks, how the tragic events unfolded, and the ways in which one devastating day changed America forever"-- Provided by publisher.
Identifiers: LCCN 2021012691 (print) | LCCN 2021012692 (ebook) | ISBN 9781663920836 (paperback) | ISBN 9781663905918 (hardcover) | ISBN 9781663905888 (pdf) | ISBN 9781663905901 (kindle edition)
Subjects: LCSH: September 11 Terrorist Attacks, 2001--Juvenile literature. | Terrorism--United States--History--21st century--Juvenile literature.
Classification: LCC HV6432.7 .M34195 2022 (print) | LCC HV6432.7 (ebook) | DDC 973.931--dc23
LC record available at https://lccn.loc.gov/2021012691
LC ebook record available at https://lccn.loc.gov/2021012692

Image Credits
Associated Press: Jim Collins, cover, Louis Lanzano, 5, Mazhar Ali Khan, 7, Shawn Baldwin, 17; Courtesy of the Federal Bureau of Investigations: 12; Getty Images: AFP/Paul J. Richards, 23, Corbis/James Leynse, 18, Craig Allen, 16; National Park Service: Flight 93 National Memorial, 26; Newscom: dpa/picture-alliance/Hubert Boesl, 20, Reuters/Jeff Christensen, 9, Reuters/Kevin Lamarque, 25, Reuters/Peter Jones, 22, Reuters/Sean Adair, 10–11, Reuters/Shannon Stapleton, 19, UPI Photo Service/Monika Graff, 21; Shutterstock: Atoly (design element), cover and throughout, gokturk_06, 13, Joseph Sohm, 14, Leena Robinson, 6, opasso, 27, QualityHD, 8; U.S. Department of Defense: Photo by Cpl. Clay Beyersdorfer, U.S. Army National Guard, 24; XNR Productions: 15

Editorial Credits
Editor: Eric Braun; Media Researcher: Svetlana Zhurkin; Production Specialist: Laura Manthe

Consultant Credits
Kevin Boyle, JD
Professor, School of Public Affairs American
University, Washington, D.C.

All internet sites appearing in back matter were available and accurate when this book was sent to press.

TABLE OF CONTENTS

Words in **bold** are in the glossary.

Early in the morning on September 11, 2001, two airplanes crashed in New York City. They hit two skyscrapers, often called the Twin Towers. The first plane hit the World Trade Center's North Tower. The second plane hit the South Tower. The planes caused big fires. The air filled with black smoke and ash. The towers could not withstand the heat. They fell to the ground.

Two more planes crashed too. One hit a building in Washington, D.C., called the Pentagon. Another crashed in Pennsylvania. People realized that the United States was under attack from **terrorists**. Terrorists use violence to scare others into doing what they want.

Almost 3,000 people were killed on 9/11. The attack led to changes in American laws and attitudes. Many Americans lived in fear of another attack. These changes to U.S. society can still be felt today.

Smoke poured from the World Trade Center on September 11, 2001, after terrorists crashed planes into the Twin Towers.

CHAPTER 1

A TUESDAY MORNING

The terrorists who attacked the United States had planned it out carefully. The attack began early on September 11, 2001. Ten terrorists came into Logan International Airport in Boston, Massachusetts. The men boarded two airplanes with hidden knives. They had chosen planes that were traveling far. Those would have the most fuel to burn in an explosion. They also chose planes with fewer passengers. That meant fewer people could fight against them.

Logan International Airport in Boston

AL-QAEDA

The attackers were members of a terrorist group called al-Qaeda. Their leader was Osama bin Laden. Bin Laden was a religious **extremist**. Bin Laden claimed the United States was trying to destroy the religion of Islam. But really, he did not follow the rules of Islam. He used religion as an excuse for violence. He did not like that the U.S. had military forces in several countries in the **Middle East**. He wanted to reduce American support of soldiers in the region.

Osama bin Laden planned and directed the 9/11 terrorist attacks.

American Airlines Flight 11 was the first plane to be attacked. At 7:59 a.m., the plane took off from Boston. It had 81 passengers and 11 crew members. It was supposed to go to Los Angeles, California. Instead, five al-Qaeda terrorists **hijacked** it. They used their knives to threaten people. They said they had a bomb. One of the men got into the **cockpit**. He knew how to fly a plane. He took control.

> **FACT**
> The Twin Towers were the two tallest buildings in New York City. They were called "twin" towers because they looked so much alike.

American Airlines Flight 11 was a large Boeing 767 airplane.

Flight 11 tore a hole into the North Tower, crashing through floors 93 to 99.

The terrorists flew the plane to New York City. At 8:46 a.m., it hit the North Tower of the World Trade Center. Everyone on the plane was killed. So were many people in the building.

At first, people thought the crash was an accident. News reporters filmed the North Tower burning. Then, a second airplane flew into the South Tower. The building was right next to the North Tower. People in the neighborhood and others watching live TV saw the second plane hit.

The second airplane was United Airlines Flight 175. It also took off from Boston. It was headed for Los Angeles. It had 56 passengers and nine crew members. Just like on Flight 11, there were five terrorists. They used knives and said they had a bomb. Then they took control of the plane.

But on Flight 175, more passengers used their phones. They made calls to tell others what was going on. Many said goodbye to their families before the plane crashed.

Hijackers flew Flight 175 toward the South Tower as the
North Tower burned. The plane hit at 9:03 a.m.

TWO MORE PLANES

After the Twin Towers were hit, airplanes continued to fly as normal for almost an hour. Then all planes were grounded.

> **FACT**
> Because of a construction project, far fewer people were in the Pentagon than usual on September 11. Thousands more could have died.

Rescue workers rushed to the Pentagon shortly after Flight 77 crashed into it at 9:37 a.m.

But American Airlines Flight 77 was already in the air. It was traveling from Washington, D.C., to Los Angeles. It had 58 passengers and six crew members. Like the other two flights, five terrorists took control. They turned the plane back toward Washington, D.C. The plane crashed into a government building called the Pentagon. Everyone on board was killed. So were 125 people in the building.

The last hijacked plane was United Airlines Flight 93. It took off from Newark International Airport in Newark, New Jersey, a few minutes before Flight 11 crashed. It was supposed to fly to San Francisco, California. On board were 37 passengers and seven crew members.

The Pentagon, named for its shape, is the headquarters of the U.S. Department of Defense.

Flight 93 had four hijackers. The men took control of the plane. They began to fly toward Washington, D.C. Most experts believe the attackers were targeting the White House or the U.S. Capitol.

THE BUILDINGS

Bin Laden chose to hit buildings that are symbols of American power. The World Trade Center represented America's wealth. It also stood for peaceful communication and trade across the world. The Pentagon is the center of the American military. The White House and Capitol are seats of the U.S. government.

The World Trade Center before 9/11

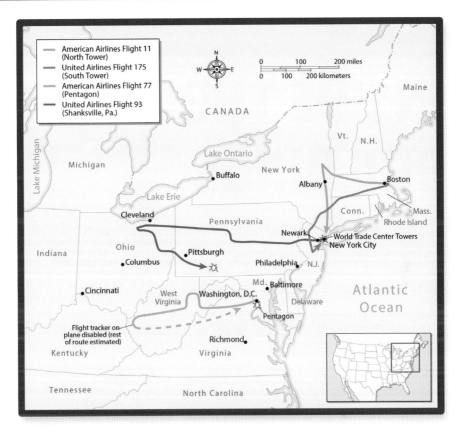

Flight paths of the four hijacked planes during the terrorist attacks

But when the terrorists took over, the passengers called their families and friends. They learned about the World Trade Center. They realized that their plane might be part of the attack.

The passengers fought back. The hijackers panicked. They lost control of the plane. Flight 93 crashed into a field in Pennsylvania. All the people on board were killed. The terrorists did not hit their target.

INSIDE THE BUILDINGS

When the planes hit the Twin Towers, about 20,000 gallons of jet fuel exploded. Both buildings were burning. The fires burned so hot that they softened the towers' steel structures.

Jet fuel caused a fiery blast when Flight 175 crashed into the South Tower.

Firefighters and other first responders risked their lives to help after the towers were hit.

Firefighters, police officers, and **emergency medical technicians** (EMTs) raced into action. These people are called **first responders**. It is their job to help in an emergency.

Thousands of rescue workers came to help. They knew the fires could not be put out easily. Still, many went inside the buildings to save people. Because of first responders, about 25,000 people escaped the towers on 9/11.

The soaring height of the Twin Towers made it difficult to rescue people after the attacks.

But the buildings were very tall. Each one had 110 floors. Some people were trapped on the highest levels. It was hard for rescuers to reach them. People had to walk down the stairs to try to get out.

Each tower had only three stairwells. Some had no working lights. Some were slippery from spilled water and fuel. Crowds of people were using the stairs. It was difficult to move quickly.

Many people decided to stay where they were. The stairwells seemed too dangerous. Some had even called 9-1-1 and were told not to move. Usually in big buildings, people are safer where they are. But in this case, the towers were not safe. By the time the rescuers realized the danger, it was too late.

FACT
Safety experts say it is not safe to use elevators when there is a fire. Always use stairs.

Survivors moving down the tower stairs

The Twin Towers were made to stand against hurricane-strength winds. They could even stay standing if a small plane hit them. But the jet fuel fires from the two large planes were very intense. The towers could not deal with the extreme heat. Columns that held up the towers were also too damaged from the impact of the planes.

Both the North and South Towers collapsed less than two hours after the planes hit. Almost everyone who was still inside was killed.

A huge cloud of dust and smoke rolled over New York City as the Twin Towers collapsed.

When the towers fell, they released a dust cloud. The dust was filled with toxic chemicals. Scientists believe that people who breathed in the dust are at risk. They are more likely to get cancer, lung diseases, and other illnesses. The dust made thousands of survivors and responders sick. Since then, hundreds of people have died from sickness caused by the dust.

First responders continued to work at the site of the fallen buildings, which became known as "Ground Zero."

CHAPTER 4

A CHANGED WORLD

September 11 affected people all over the world. Many Americans reported signs of **post-traumatic stress** in the days following the attacks. Some people went to church and prayed. Some people became very patriotic. They flew American flags. They hung signs that said, "Never Forget."

FACT

There is a long history of terrorist groups using religion, including Christianity, to do terrible things.

People gathered at a memorial for firefighters who died in the fallen towers.

President George W. Bush met with Muslim leaders at the Islamic Center of Washington, D.C., on September 17, 2001.

Many Americans blamed **Muslims** for the attacks. This was wrong and unfair. People who practice Islam are peaceful. Al-Qaeda is an extremist group. It used Islam as an excuse for violence. It does not follow the peaceful teachings of Islam.

Many Americans did not see the difference. After 9/11, they **discriminated** against Muslim people. They attacked their homes, businesses, and places of worship. Violence against Muslims is still higher than it was before 9/11.

U.S. and international forces were involved in the war in Afghanistan starting in 2001.

After 9/11, the United States sent military troops to Afghanistan. Armies from other countries joined them. Together, they fought the Taliban. The Taliban was a political group that controlled parts of Afghanistan. They had let al-Qaeda live and train there. The war weakened the Taliban. That made things harder for al-Qaeda. But it took nearly 10 years to find their leader Osama bin Laden, who had planned the attacks. He had been in hiding in Pakistan.

In the United States, President George W. Bush signed the Patriot Act. The law aimed to make it easier to stop terrorists in America. It allowed the government to find information about suspects. The U.S. government also created the Transportation Security Administration (TSA). This increased airport security.

On October 26, 2001, President Bush signed the Patriot Act into law.

The damaged part of the Pentagon was rebuilt. A **memorial** was added outside its walls. A memorial for Flight 93 was placed in the field in Pennsylvania. It stands where the plane crashed.

The Twin Towers were not rebuilt. Instead, a new building called the Freedom Tower was built in their place. Beside it stands a memorial to all who lost their lives there.

The Wall of Names was built to honor the passengers and crew of Flight 93.

The Freedom Tower, also called One World Trade Center, is the tallest building in the United States.

Many people were hurt or killed in the 9/11 attacks. But many also helped each other. They raced into burning buildings. They carried others down the tower stairs. When we remember the terrible events of 9/11, we can also choose to remember the good that people did to help each other.

TIMELINE

SEPTEMBER 11, 2001

7:59 a.m.: American Airlines Flight 11 takes off from Logan Airport in Boston.

8:14 a.m.: United Airlines Flight 175 takes off from Logan Airport in Boston. Meanwhile, Flight 11 fails to answer an order from air traffic control. The flight is most likely hijacked around this time.

8:20 a.m.: American Airlines Flight 77 takes off from Dulles Airport outside Washington, D.C.

8:42 a.m.: Flight 175 sends its last message to air traffic control. It is likely hijacked around this time. Meanwhile, United Airlines Flight 93 takes off from Newark Liberty Airport in New Jersey.

8:46 a.m.: Flight 11 crashes into the North Tower of the World Trade Center.

8:51 a.m.: Flight 77 sends its last message to air traffic control. It is likely hijacked around this time.

9:03 a.m.: Flight 175 crashes into the South Tower of the World Trade Center.

9:26 a.m.: No more flights are allowed to take off in the United States.

9:28 a.m.: Flight 93 is hijacked.

9:37 a.m.: Flight 77 crashes into the Pentagon in Arlington, Virginia.

9:57 a.m.: Passengers on Flight 93 rush toward the cockpit, trying to get control of the plane.

9:59 a.m.: The South Tower collapses, killing almost everyone inside.

10:00 a.m.: All rescuers are ordered to evacuate the North Tower.

10:03 a.m.: Flight 93 crashes in a field in Pennsylvania, killing everyone on board.

10:28 a.m.: The North Tower collapses, killing almost everyone inside.

GLOSSARY

cockpit (KOK-pit)—the area at the front of the airplane where the pilots sit and fly the plane

discriminate (dih-SKRIH-muh-nayt)—to treat a person or group unfairly because of race, religion, or another difference

emergency medical technician (ih-MUR-juhn-see MEH-dih-kuhl tek-NISH-uhn)—a person trained to treat patients before and on the way to the hospital; also called an EMT

extremist (ihk-STREE-muhst)—a person who uses violence in the name of a political or religious viewpoint

first responder (FURST rih-SPON-dur)—one of the first people to help in an accident, attack, or other emergency; includes firefighters, police officers, and EMTs

hijack (HYE-jack)—to take control of a vehicle, such as an airplane, through violence or the threat of violence

memorial (muh-MOR-ee-uhl)—something that is built or done to help people remember a person or event

Middle East (MIH-duhl EEST)—a region of the world that includes parts of western Asia, northern Africa, and southeastern Europe

Muslim (MUHZ-luhm)—a person who practices the religion of Islam

post-traumatic stress (POST-truh-mah-tik STREHS)—feelings of intense fear or worry that last long after a scary event has ended

terrorist (TER-ur-ist)—a person who uses violence and fear to further his or her cause and make others obey

READ MORE

Hunt, Jilly. *The Fight Against War and Terrorism.* Chicago: Capstone, 2018.

O'Connor, Jim. *What Were the Twin Towers?* New York: Grosset & Dunlap, 2016.

Rusick, Jessica. *September 11, 2001: Then and Now.* Minneapolis: ABDO Publishing, 2021.

INTERNET SITES

BrainPOP: September 11
brainpop.com/socialstudies/ushistory/september11th

Library of Congress: September 11, 2001, Documentary Project
loc.gov/collections/september-11th-2001-documentary-project/about-this-collection

9/11 Memorial & Museum
911memorial.org

INDEX